CAN(

David Boyle has been writing about new ideas for more than a quarter of a century. He is co-director of the New Weather Institute, a fellow of Radix and the New Economics Foundation, has stood for Parliament and is a former independent reviewer for the Cabinet Office. He is the author of *Alan Turing, Scandal* and *V for Victory,* as well as a range of other historical studies, as well as books of contemporary history like *Broke* and *Authenticity*. He lives in the South Downs.

Cancelled!

The strange, disturbing story of
the Southern Railways crisis – and
what we can do about it

David Boyle

THE REAL PRESS

www.therealpress.co.uk

Published in 2016 by the Real Press.
www.therealpress.co.uk © David Boyle

ISBN (print) 978-1534790087

ISBN (epub) 978-0993523960

Cover photograph: Summer Dean (summerdean.co.uk)

Dedicated to the customers and
staff of Southern Railway

Contents

Introduction:
The last train down
to the coast

"As a long-serving @southernrail commuter, finally radicalised by absurd circumstance, I would like to thank you."
Tweet sent to me after the blogs I wrote

The American anthropologist Polly Wiessner used to argue that the sense of reciprocity, which she studied for decades among the !Kung bushmen in southern Africa, was part of the wiring for us human beings. If she is right, we are hard-wired for give and take.

We may not fully remember this but, when it gets betrayed – when we are let down, as we so often are by the companies we shop with – we feel extremely angry. More angry than perhaps the situation demands. In the middle of the strange collapse of Southern rail services to Sussex, I remembered this and wondered.

There I was on Hayward's Heath station, when hundreds of people – maybe thousands of people around me – were showing signs, unusual in the English, of absolute rage. The third train to the coast had been cancelled. More trains were arriving, and being cancelled, as mine had been. More people were pouring onto the already crowded platform, their faces set – the sign that the English are very unhappy indeed.

"This is exactly what happened last Thursday," said a woman next to me.

"This is the third train cancelled today that I've been on," said another one. "That's another evening ruined by Southern Rail."

The staff in their yellow fluorescent jackets were calm as they directed furious passengers from platform to platform, and advised them to go via Brighton. I had already heard, at that stage, about conditions in Brighton and how the police were directing rows of shuffling, disaffected passengers trying to get trains along the coast which no longer existed. It was not a tempting prospect.

"This fucking train company," a man was saying into his mobile phone, and it was clear – in so many words – that's what other passengers were thinking too.

A train rumbled into the empty platform behind us and stopped. On impulse, I tore at the door, trying to open it with my fingers. You get desperate sometimes when you are tired and trying to get home. "This train is not stopping here," said the tannoy, in flagrant defiance of the basic facts.

"You can't do that," said a somewhat supercilious despatch staff member. "If you succeed, you'll break the door, and the train will be stuck."

In fact, of course, it was me that was stuck again. The Southern Railways crisis had increased another notch that night. Of their regular trains on the Southern network, people trying to get home to their families, up toa thirdhad been cancelled. It was hardly surprising that people were cross, as cross as the English can get when they are let down so badly by the services they pay for.

Suddenly, there was another flurry of activity. The train to the coast was moving slowly into the station. It looked dangerously full. A pregnant women ahead of me looked faint as she squeezed on. There was no question of reaching a seat. I was forced to calm a spat that broke out between two irritable passengers, one of whom was calling the other a 'do-gooder'. Like this, squeezed into this tiny space in unwilling intimacy with other members of the human race, we crawled down to the coast. Again.

Those kinds of journeys do happen sometimes, especially in the UK where the underinvestment in equipment and manpower has been chronic. But this had been the same for weeks, and appeared to be getting worse. I wrote a short blog about one conversation I had with rail staff, only to find that it had been read by more than 70,000 people in a few days. By then, the proportion of trains between London and Brighton and arriving within five minutes of their scheduled time had dropped to just 13 per cent, frustrated passengers were holding demonstrations outside the Brighton terminus. Even in leafy, respectable South Croydon, passengers abandoned on the platform were chanting: 'Where are the trains! Where are the trains!'

The whole experience made me insanely cross. Then, when the number of people reading my blog tipped over 3,000 an hour, rather scared. So many people responded with letters, comments and emails, that I suddenly knew a great deal more about Southern Railways and its unravelling than I had done a few days before. I run a small publishing enterprise. I believe that publishing should respond to the moment, and I felt this was an opportunityfor me to could show what I meant about reinventing the way publishing worked. I would find out what was really going on, and use the information I had been sent by literally hundreds of people caught up in the same affair.

This is, after all, a far more serious and, in some ways, more frightening series of events than they seemed at first.They also have important implications for the way we live. That is why I have written this book. I hope that, by explaining what is really going on, and suggesting things we might do about it, that I will have been able to make a small difference. Not least of which, a small difference to my train journeys to London and back.

I
The crisis

"The thing is, I don't believe this stuff about staff shortages."
My words to the platform staff on Southern which led directly to this book

Those were the words I used to the member of platform staff I had asked about trains to London. I was at a different station to the one I usually use, and – to be honest – I didn't realise that was what I thought until I said it. The phrase was almost magic. It released the door like the words 'open sesame'.

I had asked why there were no trains on their running timetable to London at all. It was odd, even by the low standards of Southern Railways over the previous weeks, to have them take the trains they could not run off the timetable altogether. Usually, they just marked them as having been cancelled.

"Well," she said. "It's still the problem with staff shortages."

It was then that I finally expressed my disbelief. Only a few weeks before, Southern had been claiming that the problems had been caused by unprecedented sickness amongst the train crew. Now they appeared to be saying that the train crew did not exist at all. I asked myself also why any competent company should experience a sudden, prolonged and catastrophic staff shortage, immediately after the short train strike in April, that prevented them from running a large chunk of the trains they are contracted to run?

"You're right," she said. "It isn't true."

"So what is the truth?" I said hopefully.

"I can't tell you that because I would be sacked."

I had to question a number of other staff members to find out – and I had the chance to see a number of them that day because it was so difficult getting to London, despite the scheduled two direct trains every hour. The answer, it seemed at the time, was that the company had banned the railway staff involved in the two strikes from doing overtime, to stop them clawing back their lost money. This was not quite accurate – the truth, as we shall see, was even stranger.

What was clear was that Southern were relying perhaps more than they should on the willingness of train crews to do overtime. Without overtime, the train service becomes impossible. The result was chaos – a wholly unreliable service which at weekends and in the eveningswas becoming dangerously overcrowded.

I have a blog which was once daily, but is now weekly, so I wrote up the conversation the next day and posted it. I was staggered to see it had been read by about 2,000 people within a few hours. By the time the figure had reached 60,000, I was also unnerved. I knew how angry I was, but the thought of tens of thousands of people being angry because of their cancelled and exhausting journeys home, and focusing that anger in my direction (though not actually at me) was actually frightening.

Then the messages started to arrive. I had texts, emails and tweets, some long and detailed, some short and emotional, from passengers, drivers and platform staff. I had short messages full of swearwords. I had long messages from company chairmen, sitting on motionless trains outside Clapham Junction, explaining that – as far as they could see – Southern Railways was unravelling before their very eyes.

The prevailing message from most of the passengers was a combination of rage and powerlessness. "It's depressing and scary," said one of my messages. "The majority of us commuters are with you, the staff of Southern Rail. We are slowly but surely understanding what's really going on. Just a quick glance at Twitter shows that the travelling public understand it is Southern management and the DfT (Department for Transport) rather than the customer facing staff that are to blame. Now we just need to figure out what, if anything, can be done before the entire south coast rail infrastructure grinds to a complete halt."

"We need to make this widely known and to protest in some way!" said another.

A third put it like this: "My attempts to complain to GTR directly have simply been ignored and as a fare paying passenger I feel that to GTR regard me as just an inconvenience. It feels like our rights are being undermined as much as it is for their employees. The situation is beyond unacceptable. Is there anything else we can do?"

The snag is that the English middle classes are not good at protest. They don't really know what to do when the establishment messes them around. More on that later.

"I was so f****d off with the shambles that was yesterday and the fact that I saw someone faint in front of me that I called my local paper on the way home – this is now the most read news story on their website today," wrote another correspondent, in this case, Ben Lambert.

"It was so packed around the doors that, when we were nearing Hove, the woman next to me collapsed and fainted onto the floor," he told the *Brighton Argus*. "We got her onto her feet and she was dizzy and confused and I was getting out and people were trying to create some space for her."

Another message, complaining about the picture of a slave ship I had unwisely used to illustrate my blog, said: "When you become troublesome to SR (Southern Railways), you are not thrown overboard to drown or to the sharks and you are just figuratively chained to the passenger next to you."

I had one email that particularly made me think. "I, too, am a hapless Southern commuter to/from London and was struck by the 'staff shortages' blanket excuse of late," said Rachel. "So I checked Southern's vacancies webpage (hey, I'll be a train driver!) and they don't seem to be hiring much at the moment. Odd, isn't it?"

Fascinated, I looked up the vacancies page myself and, sure enough, there were just five of them, and none of them were for train crews. The occasional responses of MPs and ministers implied there was huge recruitment going on. The statement by Southern Railways' ultimate owner, Go-Ahead, which blamed the crisis for their share price dropping, said that they were "having to invest additional resources". Where were they?

It was explained to me by Go-Ahead, who I called, that their costs were mainly people, trains and fuel. Most of the extra resources brought in to tackle the crisis have been people, mainly traffic controllers. Part of the difficulty as I understood it is that training drivers takes time, and they also have to train them again to drive the new trains, the gleaming Class 700 trains, built in Germany and waiting permission to use. They also cost around £100,000 to train.

Even so, I couldn't resist applying to be a train driver myself, but it was hardly easy. There was no button to press to apply for a job which is not advertised. I had to hang on the line for about twenty minutes before someone answered. They advised me to send an email to their recruitment address. I got an automatic reply:

"This email address is not monitored."

Despite this small failure, I am sure that the driver recruitment programme existed, but – if my own experience has been anything to go by – they are not actively recruiting now.

This is the first time in this book I have had to name Southern's operators, Govia Thameslink Railway – henceforth known by the acronym GTR, of whom more later. It was the surprise in 2014 that awaited GTR when they took over the Thameslink franchise that they had fewer drivers than they had come to expect, which led to the recruitment drive. In fact they recruited over 200 drivers, of whom about 70 are due for the Southern area.

They are arriving for work now at the rate of four or five a month, and their absence now is a kind of grumbling background staff shortage, which doesn't explain the current crisis but does rather inform it.

The other peculiar story that I kept hearing was that there were staff available waiting in depots, or – even worse – turning up to drive a train, only to find that it had been cancelled because of 'staff shortages'. I have had a number of messages, from drivers and guards as well, testifying to the truth of this.

Some Southern staff clearly regarded the blog I wrote as an attempt to tell the truth. "My God," wrote one. "I am so pleased to see this. Finally the truth, but I can report it's only part of the sad and sorry story!" The message went on:

"Trains are being cancelled at an alarming rate despite train crew (driver and guard) being in place and booked to work the trains. This is happening dozens of times per day! I know because it has happened to me. Turn up ready and willing to work the train, only to be told it has been cancelled due to no train crew. Due to the court injunction on Aslef drivers, we can't even openly express our anger at this. If we do so it might be found in so called e-search that is being conducted on driver's personal phones and computers looking for evidence of incitement to strike! Make no mistake, GTR are coming after their own staff like the KGB and Stasi!"

Another driver wrote to me like this:

"A few weeks ago, I was at a station waiting to leave. I was then told the train was cancelled due to no guard, [but] the guard was on the train waiting to go. He had been sent from another depot to cover this train. When I contacted control to ask what was happening they said: 'Well, nobody told us he was there which is why it's been cancelled'. On this occasion, I managed to persuade them to run the train for the sake of the passengers."

There is a high court injunction on the rail unions not to encourage strikes, and clearly this is unusual – but, apart from that, and the obvious nervousness of Southern staff – I have seen no evidence of the KGB so far. Though I have met staff members who fell foul of the company for posting on Facebook. Nor in the end is the phenomenon of the crews turning up to drive cancelled trains quite as mysterious as it seems.

If you believe, as the rail unions clearly do, in the absolute malevolence of the company, then this is conspiracy. The truth is more mundane: the Southern control centre at Three Bridges has been almost overwhelmed by the number of cancelled and redirected trains.

When they see how many staff they have available at the beginning of the day, they designate which trains they will need to cancel. But the job of persuading crews to come in on their days off to drive the cancelled trains falls to the depots. The two bits don't communicate very well, so sometimes they turn up to drive cancelled trains. The rostering system is phenomenally complex. It is cock-up not conspiracy. It is a symptom of poor communication between the local depots and the control centre, a clear sign of over-centralisation.

Not that this makes passengers any less cross.

There is a difference between now and days gone by, when train companies would keep spare drivers on the roster in case something happened. This kind of sensible precaution, building in spare capacity, still happens under the rule of GTR, but not nearly so much. Because, far too often, the spare drivers are used to avoid paying overtime to cover for predictable absences, not to cover for last minute unpredictable ones.

It hardly seems surprising that, when the unpredictable events happen – accidents, sudden illness, disruption at London Bridge again – the spare capacity has already been used.

This is, at least, the interpretation of some of

the crews who contacted me.

With me so far? Then two events happened in April and May which turned an under-capacity into a crisis.

In April was the first two-day rail strike over driver-only trains. In May, the timetable changed and there were more 40 trains to run. Most of the new drivers had not yet arrived and the company had been planning to cover the extra work from the existing crews. The recruitment of guards had not been happening with quite the same enthusiasm, because GTR wants to do away with the role – but it was the remaining, overstretched guards who had to face the fury of the customers once the delays became intolerable.

Part of the problem is that these extra stresses have caused more sickness and more absences. There has also been a serious drop in morale, which everyone recognises can have an impact on sick leave. "The reason why we are not working rest days and overtime (as a driver) is because the work place is so utterly depressing we can't face being there any more than we have to and because GTR have fostered a deep seated hatred that will take many years to clear away unless GTR go," wrote one of my driver informants.

Then there is the rise in sick leave. This is the official reason for the current crisis, so it needs a bit of unpacking. In the immediate aftermath of the two-day strike at the end of April, the number of sick days taken by guards rose by around 27 a day to about 41 a day. This has now drifted back down. But it is what the rail minister calls the RMT's 'work to rule', though there is really no evidence for that. How simple it would all be if someone had caused this chaos *deliberately*. But it is worse than that.

This is what one of the guards told me:

"I have found that the way this company have treated their staff (I work for them) by taking away the travel passes from their partners and children truly disgusting. In the pursuit of reducing costs as demanded by McNulty, ordered by the DfT and executed by senior GTR management, morale is at rock bottom. The company's response to the situation has at best been cold and uncaring. They wonder why morale is low then issue letters hoping that bridges can be built between the company and staff. They justify taking travel passes off families of staff by telling staff that 'we did warn you that strike action comes with consequences '. By doing this the company has destroyed the goodwill (overtime) that it has relied on for many years to run the service. This goodwill will never be recovered whilst the current situation is happening."

There is, in this message, evidence of just how difficult it is for outsiders to get to the bottom of the truth. More on the McNulty Report in a moment, but it is certainly true that the company threatened to take away the traditional free family travel passes and car park permits if staff took part in the strike in April. They did, and the result has been that some staff have found it harder to get to work. They have had to pay to park all day or get to work on the disrupted trains. It has been tough and expensive. It is hardly surprising that borderline sick staff stay at home.

"You can imagine the kind of strains that placed on young families with children who relied on these passes to get to school," one guard told me.

Then there is the critical business of the sanctions which followed the two strikes in April and May, of which more in the next chapter. Because we are now getting close to the nub of the matter. This is how one driver put it:

> "All train crew want to do their job and get you
> the passenger to where you want to be. It's the
> most satisfying feeling in their work to roll in to
> your destination on time. GTR are finding ever
> more creative ways to prevent this in the hopes
> that you the travelling public will turn against
> us. I am delighted to see that this horrid plan is
> not working. My job is now an embarrassment.
> Well done, GTR."

That message, perhaps more than any other, revealed to me the depth of disaffection in the company – and not just amongst the ordinary staff, but the managers too.

I have had messages from platform staff saying how grateful they are to the public for supporting them when passengers lose their tempers with them. Perhaps most revealing was this one, from a passenger:

> "The biggest evil of it all is that the so called
> GTR is a ghost. We can neither see nor touch
> them. And this they know. The staff are being
> used as a blooded shield, intentionally bashed
> about time and time again. But we, the daily

commuters, are the wood that makes up that shield and we are loyal to those that serve us. The hard working and genuine conductors, drivers, station staff who are being mercilessly put on the front line of what is proving to be a shameless and spiteful battle. Man up GTR. Get a grip and get on with it. For the sake of us all."

This was the element of the situation that struck me most, and made me most angry. Here were the platform staff, plunged day after day into the most dangerous crowd situations, without proper support or proper information, with some extremely angry people. But where were their senior managers? Whatever happened to the Tom Peters concept MBWA (Management By Walking Around)? It was not just the passengers who had been abandoned, it was the staff too, and it used to be one of the essential elements of management was to instil that sense of responsibility and leadership. The staff seem to have that in abundance, but it can't be inexhaustible.

Dyan Crowther, the GTR chief operating officer, told me she had been to Victoria (she works at GTR's office in Monument Street behind London Bridge), but the sense that managers are behind their staff seems to be seriously missing.

"In the twenty years on this job, I have never known anything like it," wrote one staff member. "On a daily basis, staff are bearing the brunt of passengers understandable frustrations at a crap service. Even I have been on the receiving end of things whilst in uniform on my way to work. On this occasion, another passenger stepped in and helped me out. Clearly this company does not care about its staff...

> "The senior management should be ashamed of themselves by the way they are treating their staff. I am ashamed to wear the uniform of the company and to work for them. I'm seriously thinking of quitting."

A message from another member of the platform staff, sent from his company email, said he had in fact resigned in disgust that very day. "Until today I was one of the put upon platform staff," they wrote. "I have just resigned. I'm fed up with the continual abuse we receive on a daily basis and this company's refusal to do anything about it..."

What I see every time I travelled was not the boorish, destructive, recalcitrant workforce that government ministers were painting, but brave, resourceful, patient staff, explaining to passengers what they believed was happening from moment to moment, with no information and under the most enormous pressure. Day after day, I see them heroically coping with the stress, never getting cross or raising their voices as the anger of customer begins to ignite. Never criticising GTR or its managers. I did not see the company directors there alongside them; maybe they were there – I know managers have been there – but they were not obvious to me.

On one occasion, I was trying to get anywhere south of Clapham Junction in the evening, and was stuck at Victoria Station, being herded by tannoy announcements three times between motionless trains for nearly an hour. The moment the extremely crowded train moved, the guard came on the loudspeaker with a comedy routine so practised, so charming and so honest, that everyone was smiling within moments.

"Well – that *was* a long wait," he said. "Do you know, I've been waiting an *hour* to take this train out!" It was so human, so expert, that it seemed as if it must have been trained, but I am almost sure it was not. It was just a company employee using his initiative and lightening the situation in the most imaginative way. I took my hat off to him and hope he was thanked profusely by the company, but rather suspect he was not.

It is worth asking why people get so cross. It isn't as if this is a public service, like the ambulances, where lives are at stake – though there are rather obvious risks from crowded trains and platforms. When the delayed trains crawl through Sussex, they are doing so through some of the most beautiful countryside in England. It is not as if this is taking place in a concrete jungle (though there is Gatwick, of course).

It is because these are people who are either trying to get to work or to get back from work to see their families. When they are prevented from doing so, it makes them angry. When they are prevented from doing so in new ways, evening after evening, it becomes enraging. They have paid maybe more than £400 a month to go regularly from London to Brighton every working day. They want to get home. Their treatment at the hands of Southern seems at the time like a betrayal, and it is one.

I find myself calming down once I get home, but I am still exhausted. What I wanted to do in the evening is now impossible. I have been imprisoned effectively in a can for some hours, against my will. Of course I am angry.

This is one message I received which will have to stand for many others. It outlines the disaffection amongst GTR's passengers, and the cynicism this kind of failure encourages:

"For the level of shameful performance to have gone on for so long without action or redress means the DfT [Department for Transport] must be complicit. I simply do not understand how this situation is allowed to continue for an essential public service. It is so abundantly clear that they only care about profit and keeping operating costs at bare minimum. That is why we experience stock and staff shortages. They treat staff and customers with abysmal disdain. MPs, who appeared to be outraged and supportive of the travelling public earlier in the year, now appear to have fallen silent. It's a conspiracy and it's a prime example of how modern Britain operates purely in the interest of private wealth at public expense. It's a scandal and needs to be fully exposed."

More about the politics of this later. But it is worth outlining the most worrying implication. Train transport is a privatized public service, using management methods and with a relationship to the government which is repeated across most, if not all, public services. The worry is that, in the same way, this same chaos will spread to every public service, using the same structures, techniques, centralized targets and staff relations (they treat their staff from a distance, as if they were young offenders).

If this happens on the railways, why not soon everywhere else?

II
The story

"I wanted to contact you more on a personal level to say I am ashamed of how we at Southern are performing. I am completely at a loss as to why this remains the case and indeed it is deteriorating."
Message sent to me by a guard

The Brighton Belle was famous for its kippers. Laurence Olivier would take a leisurely breakfast back to his home in Ashurst in Sussex on the train after a West End triumph, reading the theatre reviews. The train began life in June 1934 and most of the brown and cream Pullman carriages – the only electric Pullman carriages in the world – survived the war, holed up in the Crystal Palace High Level Station, now a housing estate.

The Brighton Belle only took an hour to go the 51 miles from Victoria to Brighton, and it left every day at noon, pulling into the seaside at one o'clock on the dot. Along with the Golden Arrow boat train to Paris, it was the jewel in the crown of the old Southern Railways. It lasted until the 1970s.Southern's successors have not managed to keep up the reputation for luxury.

So wander back with me a moment, if you will, to the great days of the Southern. It is worth remembering because, although it is a different shape to the GTR franchise now – which covers the Great Northern franchise as well, and rather bizarrely has a registered office in Newcastle – it is not entirely dissimilar.

The other difference is that the old Southern Railways used to go as far as Cornwall, operating out of the biggest and most complex of all the London railway terminals, at Waterloo. It also had a reputation for extreme efficiency, which none of the other Big Four railway companies, operating from 1923 to 1948, managed to attain.

The success was partly the triumph of a great railway leader, Sir Herbert Walker, and the journalist J. B. Elliot who took over from him and who masterminded Southern's distinctive advertising (the little boy looking up at the train driver in his cab is still with us). It was Walker who managed to forge all the companies that made up Southern into one unit, symbolised by smashing a whole between the two parallel stations at Victoria.

He also gave all Southern staff one uniform, including a distinctive red tie which doubled as a flag to pull off and wave, like Bobbie in *The Railway Children*, in train emergencies.

Within three years of their launch, Southern faced their own industrial action when their staff walked out in 1926 in the General Strike. On the final day, Walker announced that he was reinstating his workforce. In return, the rail unions promised not to strike again without negotiations first.

Southern handed over to British Rail in 1948 with its reputation intact, its ferries still sailing and its kippers still on the menu.

Fast forward four decades, to the tail end of the Thatcher government, and there was still little appetite for privatising the railways. It was the unexpected victory of John Major in the 1992 election that propelled it to the top of the political agenda. The idea of selling the railways was rushed, to get it done in one parliament, and confused. It was dubbed the "poll tax on wheels" by the Conservative critic and railway buff Robert Adley MP.

The real weakness was the decision to hand the track and stations over to a new private entity called Railtrack, which had almost no expertise, and very little interest in the technical side. Key engineering skills, built up over decades at British Rail were dissipated and lost.

Railtrack was persuaded to 'sweat their assets' by management consultancies which knew even less about railways than they did. The result was the panic that followed the Hatfield rail crash in 2000 and Railtrack's forcing into receivership. The continuing issue about rail privatisation was set out clearly by John Hendy QC in his report on the Ladbroke Grove and Southall crashes:

"A single organisation, the railway, cannot be satisfactorily run exclusively by legal contractual relations," he wrote. "Tightly specified contracts are incapable of creating co-operative commitment to safety: no contract can ever eliminate the space for parties not to pursue its terms wholeheartedly."

Not every enterprise needs to be centralised and run from a government department. Far from it. But if it is divided up, there still needs to be some measure of co-operation across responsibilities and sectors to make it effective, some sharing of information, some sense of goodwill.

The contract culture we have chosen to run our services is not very effective at shaping this. That is one of the factors now in the unravelling of Southern Railways.

The word 'privatisation' has had a chequered history. It was actually coined as 'reprivatisation' by the Nazi Party in the 1930s, as a way of handing over government functions to loyal party officials. The phrase was then borrowed by the great management writer Peter Drucker in 1969, proposing that governments use the talent in other sectors to deliver some of their objectives. "Government is a poor manager .... It has no choice but to be 'bureaucratic," he wrote.

That was the basic idea that was taken up by Conservative thinkers in the 1970s. Sir Keith Joseph's Centre for Policy Studies produced a pamphlet in 1975 which set out the case: "There is now abundant evidence that state enterprises in the UK have not served well either their customers, or their employees, or the taxpayer, for when the state owns, nobody owns and when nobody owns, nobody cares." It was a powerful proposition.

In the event, when Margaret Thatcher came to power four years later, she had other things on her mind. There was some tiptoeing towards privatisation – the sale of Cable & Wireless and British Aerospace in 1981 – but it wasn't until after the Falklands war and her 1983 election victory that she grasped the sheer power of the privatisation idea. It was obvious to anyone who tried to use them that the nation's telephone boxes were largely out of order, and so the privatisation of British Telecom in 1984 was a popular move. As many as 2.3m people brought shares.

Three years later, the Treasury had earned £24 billion, and the sale of British Gas provided four per cent of public spending for 1986/7. The idea of privatising state industries had spread to France and the USA and Canada. Even Cuba and China were testing it out. The merchant bank Rothschilds had set up a special unit to organise privatisations, under the future Conservative frontbencher John Redwood, and Conservative theorists were muttering darkly about selling off the Atomic Energy Authority and the BBC.

In fact, at the time, selling nuclear power stations proved to be the thin end of the wedge. It became clear that, actually, no amount of spin could disguise the fact that they weren't economic. Now of course, these decisions are made by the French government on our behalf.

The original impetus to sell BT was partly to find private investment for telecoms and partly because of Drucker's idea, that private companies were more efficient. By 1985, that was just one of the benefits – it was also supposed to help employees get a stake in the business, provide wider share ownership and reduce the role of the public sector. All those happened, though one of Redwood's team, another future Conservative star Oliver Letwin, said that actually there was very little evidence for the idea that privatised companies were more efficient. A quick glance at the private health corporations of the USA is enough to cast doubt on this one – their health system costs 13.6 per cent of GDP, while the public British system costs half that, mainly because a quarter of health spending in the USA goes on the bureaucracy of billing, negotiation and payments.

Even so, there was a logic about the idea that seemed to add up. Privatising public services would break those bureaucratic straitjackets, and get a new entrepreneurial energy about the place. There would be a focus on customers. Things would happen. There would be enterprise and imagination. The trouble is that isn't what happened. The early privatisations led to dramatic increases in effectiveness but, after that, things slowed down. Private corporate giants turned out to be as inflexible and hopelessly unproductive (at least as far as the customers were concerned) as the public corporate giants: they just provided fewer jobs.

Often the cost remained much the same. In fact, as it turned out, many privatised services are as sclerotic, inhuman and monstrous as their predecessors were.

The Conservative theorist Ferdinand Mount realised this as early as 1987. "It is becoming increasingly clear that the regulators have no teeth and the operators no conscience," he wrote, and so it proved. In fact, the privatised operators were determined to become as much like governments as they could. Railtrack – the original privatised owner of the infrastructure – ran a unit of 25 staff just to battle with the Rail Regulator.

A decade later, and the supposedly efficient private utilities are largely in the grip of a concept of efficiency that is being swept away in smaller, more entrepreneurial businesses. There are phalanxes of call centres, targets and standards, just as the public sector has. They are as inflexible as any nationalised industry used to be. If the police are spending more time on forms than on the beat, then Soviet-style command-and-control is alive and well in the private sector, just when it was supposed to have been consigned to history with the Berlin Wall.

"We are committed to a market economy at the national level, and a non-market, centrally planned, hierarchically managed economy within most corporations," wrote the *Observer* business columnist Simon Caulkin.

So Peter Drucker was wrong. As it turned out, big companies and big contracts necessarily become bureaucratic too. The point wasn't that private was better than public, it was that small was better than big, because small allowed for informality, give and take, flexibility and all those elements that big, complex organisations are so bad at. That is why research shows that results and behaviour are better at smaller schools than bigger schools, that less hospitals cost less per patient than big ones, that small police forces catch more criminals than big ones. I could go on.

It was even Drucker who provided the clue. Anyone can be an entrepreneur if the organisation is structured to encourage them. "The most entrepreneurial, innovative people behave like the worst time-serving bureaucrat or power-hungry politician six months after they have taken over the management of a public service institution," he wrote. And so it proved.

Yet these lessons have not been learned in government. In fact, in recent years, there have been efforts to get back to John Major's original vision for rail privatisation, back to the original shape of the rail companies as they were until nationalisation in 1948. That made some sense – each company would be big enough to have its own integrated rail maintenance teams and knowhow.Big made more sense to them: big meant integration and the ability to raise even greater capital sums, at lower costs. It meant efficiency, or at least it seemed to.

The trouble is that, as we have seen at Southern, there are such things as economies of scale, but they are very rapidly overtaken by diseconomies of scale, in ways in which these monster companies seem incapable of discerning – because their numerical reporting systems are not designed to recognise them.

The background to the current crisis at Southern was a report by Sir Roy McNulty, launched in May 2011, and called *Realising the Potential of GB Rail*. The report belongs to the first push towards 'austerity' by the UK government, and the open-minded attempt to see what kind of cost savings in public spending might be possible.

The real problem for rail is that it is growing so fast, especially in London and the south east, where the population is growing so fast, that it needs to think more creatively about keeping costs down.

McNulty's solution was what he called 'whole systems'. To really innovate, you have to be able to see the transport system as a whole – not necessarily to centralise services – but to see clearly where they push costs onto each other. He wanted an integrated team at the Department of Transport, which – five years on – shows no sign of emerging. The besetting sin of English government has been to go for the cheapest option in any situation, and the response to McNulty has been no exception.

There have been new train designs and new trains, but other kinds of IT solutions that could put passengers more in control have been more difficult. The new trains have no wifi systems, and no other IT innovations which might potentially tackle some of the information difficulties that Southern has been facing.

The key point about McNulty is that the report

focused attention on staff. Staff, fuel and trains are really the only major costs for transport companies. The new trains are more energy efficient, and they are classed as capital spending anyway, so that only left the staff. And there is a continuing nervousness inside the civil service, especially during Conservative governments – and especially at the Department for Transport – about what the notorious railway unions might do to them.

UK management has been terrified of organised labour – though they are shadows of their former selves – and have failed to rise to the challenge of inspiring and leading staff as their continental counterparts have done. More on this later.

So the stage was set for another pointless confrontation. When Peter Wilkinson, a transport consultant now head of franchising for the Department for Transport, spoke at a public meeting in Croydon at the start of the year, he told militants (it isn't clear how he defined it) to "get the hell out of my industry".

He appears to have been referring to the coming dispute about driver-only trains. The government has designated the GTR franchise as one which will do away with the safety role of guards. That means a repeat of the depressing series of confrontations in key UK industries.

Charles Horton, GTR's chief executive, played a similar tough guy role in the old Connex franchise. Dyan Crowther has been involved in disputes before. There is not a tradition of close working relationships between managers and staff in the railways.

Perhaps the real problem is that GTR is too big an operation to be able to deal with face-to-face issues. It is run at a distance by the Go Ahead group, and by people who believe that big works effectively and that IT and distant systems and processes can replace human interaction. The result has been the kind of punitive, prison governor relationship between GTR and its staff which has led to the current impasse. Big organisations are necessarily less human and more complex. They don't nurture, they don't innovate and they don't lead effectively. In that respect, GTR is the quintessential 'absent company'.

Before we pin the whole problem at the door of the DfT and GTR, we can't really let two other players off the hook.

The first is the RMT union, which seems to be unhelpfully wedded to the old-fashioned symbols of socialist revolt. Their case is systematically undermined by their inability to campaign effectively, their irritatingly boorish interventions and their failure to fall back on anything except pretty self-destructive strike action, which certainly fails to help passengers. As I write, they are about to fling away the moral high ground by battering the passengers again.

But they are right about one thing. The idea that these customer service personnel will still be there after say six years is pretty delusory. Southern stations, and Southern carriages, will then be echoing ghosts of their former selves.

The other player is much more shadowy. The owners of GTR is the Go Ahead Group, which – very quietly and without much publicity – stand behind the mess at Victoria Station every evening.

Go Ahead was originally a bus company from North East England, founded only in 1987, which got big through bus privatisation. It still runs buses, in fact most of its profits come from buses, and its registered office is still in Newcastle, but its actual corporate headquarters is in Matthew Parker Street in the City of London. There the company is chaired by Andrew Allner, a former partner at accountants PricewaterhouseCoopers.

He is supported in this by a number of non-executive directors. They include: Katherine Innes Ker, a former financial analyst and now chair of the Mortgage Advice Bureau, and is a former molecular biologist. Also Nick Horler, a former chief executive of Scottish Power, and Adrian Ewer, a former chief executive of builders John Laing.

Together, Go Ahead now has 26,000 employees and a turnover of £3.2 billion. They are run by chief executive David Brown, who earns a salary and bonuses worth more than £2m. RMT points out that his pay package, together with that of the former finance director Keith Down's, was more than the £2m in fines GTR incurred during 2014.

Go Ahead presides over a strange network of interlocking ventures and joint ventures, which mean that, in some form or another, Govia – a subsidiary holding company of Go Ahead – is involved in the management of most of the railways in south east England, covering about a third of all UK railway journeys. But it is their joint venture GTR which concerns us here.

GTR (Govia Thameslink Railway) is 65 per cent owned by Go Ahead. The rest is owned by the big French transport operator Keolis. They recruited

Charles Horton to run it from the failed operator Connex – though he had experience as managing director of Southeastern and with the London Underground. The stage was set for the next phase of rail franchising.

The Department of Transport had decided it wanted to achieve two things in the south east in particular. They wanted to radically reduce costs, and needed to tame the unions to do so. They also believed that the high investment needed at London Bridge (£6 billion) would need a big operator to manage the complexity and the debts.

They had begun to think big in other ways too. When John Major's government first embraced the idea of privatising the railways which – until she was stuck on a motionless train on the way to Blackpool – Margaret Thatcher had rejected, he had imagined returning to the days of pre-nationalisation, with SR, LNER, LMS and GWR fighting it out in their browns and greens.

It was a romantic vision, and conservative in a way that John Major was, but it didn't quite add up. The EU trade regulators were insisting that the track and stations should be hived off and there was little real competition between the Big Four – except perhaps to speed from London to Scotland. Now, officials began to wonder if bigger and integrated might make more sense than fragmented and competing.

It happened to coincide with a period when, despite the rhetoric, competition was not very important in contemporary Conservative thinking. It was a moment when the whole purpose of privatisation became getting services off the government's balance sheet – when 'choice' began to mean, not choice, but *private*. Even the bare bones of competition in the days of the Big Four has now disappeared, given that both the West Coast and the East Coast main lines are now in the hands of Virgin Trains. If you don't like Virgin, then hard luck.

That was how the franchise for London and its surrounding countryside came to be dominated by one company.

GTR is the jewel in Go Ahead's crown. It operates three rail franchises together, Thameslink, Great Northern and Southern and will do so until 2021, unless they break the terms of their contract in some way – or unless the government finally gives up on their inability to run trains on time or to get on with their own staff. Their owners Govia also run the London Midland and Southeastern franchises. There is something rather incestuous about the world of trains.

Govia has its own board, under Go Ahead's chief executive David Brown. So does GTR under chief executive Charles Horton. It probably makes sense to name the other GTR directors. They are Dyan Crowther, mentioned before, who is the tough-minded chief operations officer. Also Wilma Allan (chief finance officer), Stu Cheshire, Andy Bindon...

They work at 24 Monument Street, recently fitted out for its expanding headquarters staff. "The design process included challenging the client's current working culture and providing a more agile workspace," wrote their interior decor consultants. "The introduction of a communal staff refectory, stand up meeting areas, high backed sofas and a flexible meeting suite allow staff to undertake daily activities in a tailor made environment."

This is where the fraught issue of Driver Only Operation comes in. It amounts to another acronym (DOO) and it is a controversial business. About 60 per cent of GTR's operation is already driver-only, so this is not a revolutionary idea. The Department of Transport is determined that this should be a way of cutting costs, and have decided to test the idea in four more areas. Anyone who lives in the Scotrail area will know that the clashes between management have begun there in earnest.

The official's unspoken, but rather obvious plan, is that this franchise will determine the principle that guards are unnecessary, by ending their safety duties and turning them into on-board supervisors. Then – after 2021 – the trains will presumably be stripped of their customer supervisors, and all trains will follow the lonely Thameslink model.

GTR have made as good an offer to the guards as they seem likely to achieve, involving no job losses until 2021, higher wages and this new role – leaving the business of shutting the doors to the drivers and their new CCTV systems, already built into the latest trains from Germany. They will be better off if they accept it. So why don't they? It is because they don't really believe it.

Neither side of the argument is quite convincing about the safety implications. The RMT union published a safety dossier, but you have to say that the principle is pretty established. On the other hand, one glance at the rather empty safety investigation by the Rail Safety and Standards Board reveals just how little research has actually been done – the small print reveals that their report on diver-only involved only four face-to-face interviews. Whenever there have been accidents on platforms, it tends to involve driver-only trains.

I would not dismiss the ambition to make railways cheaper to run. It means they can be sustainable in the years ahead, when it seems likely that the economy will not grow very much – and may actually be steady. Economies matter. But a totally efficient, technocratic railway that leaves passengers entirely at the mercy of machines to buy their tickets, keep them safe on platforms and on trains, guide them when there are difficulties, dangers or disruption, is not very attractive either. People don't like dealing with robots, and when companies behave like robots – without the ability to use information or common sense effectively – it sends a shiver down the spine. It isn't human.

But there is another problem. Passengers certainly might welcome the redeployment of ticket staff onto the platform with touchscreens to help people, help old people or disabled people on and off trains. They might well welcome guards as on-board customer service managers. But when the company imposes these contracts in August (or possibly later), it means that they will no longer *need* guards during disruption.

There may be safety issues, as the union says. We have all rescued old people – as I have – trapped in doors on underground trains, when the driver can't see them. There may be solutions here too. But nobody, not staff or customers, believes that these on-platform or on-board customer service people will still be there after the next round of franchises after 2021.

In that respect, the company is not being entirely honest with us. The Department for Transport is fully aware of what they are doing – they are busily taking humans out of the train business.

Where guards have lost their safety or train despatch roles, as they did on the Gatwick Express service, their customer service replacements never lasted long. That is the direction of travel the Department for Transport appears to have chosen, though some of the train operators – South West Trains, for example – are recruiting guards as a way of advertising the safety and comfort of their service.

It hardly helps GTR's case that they are also getting rid of station staff and ticket offices all over the Southern region at the same time. It makes sense to take ticket staff out from behind their glass walls and onto the platforms to help people with the intransigent ticket machines.

The trouble is that these on-platform customer supervisors don't seem to be appearing either. In fact, a number of stations now have no presence at all. It goes without saying that passengers would prefer to be safer than sorry, and – although they might trade in more safety for slightly cheaper fares – they do not want to rattle around in a giant human machine without human interaction, especially as the technology is never foolproof and is often rather second rate.

The point here is that the integration of the GTR region, from north London suburbs right down to the south coast, is designed partly to force through a driver-only future. It is a difficult integration to achieve, with a system that badly needs renewal and the badly-handled changes at London Bridge to finish – and then, on top of everything else, they are expected to cajole their guards into accepting this new role, and to batter the rail unions into accepting it too.

For generations, UK managers have banged

their heads away at this kind of problem. German or American managers have managed to achieve supportive, mutually respectful relations with their workforce, but – especially when governments get involved – senior managers seem to revert to a brutish, prison officer style, without apparently understanding how ineffective it is. Threats and bluster never work very well. They are extremely uninspiring and there is more than a whiff of class consciousness about it, though the directors of Go Ahead are far removed from the front line and may not even be fully aware of it. There is an officer class acceptance of the brutality of the relations between NCOs and staff, a blind snobbery which simply wastes time and money. And nowhere more so than in the incestuous world of railways.

One of the features of a failed policy is the way that both sides in the dispute buttress their case with out-of context quotations from the other side. The GTR spokespeople are quick to slip you quotations from the June 2016 Aslef newsletter which says about the driver-only dispute: "It's time to draw a line, dig the trenches, and prepare for war."

In the same way, the RMT will slip you (and have slipped me) notes of what the Department for

Transport's director of train franchising Peter Wilkinson said at a public meeting in Croydon in January (referred to above):

> "I'm furious about it and it has got to change – we have got to break them. They have all borrowed money to buy cars and got credit cards. They can't afford to spend too long on strike and I will push them into that place. They will have to decide if they want to give a good service or get the hell out of my industry."

Wilkinson's words raised eyebrows in the railway press, though he issued an apology for them afterwards. Journalists assumed he had spoken out of turn – maybe he had got out of bed the wrong side – and that this did not represent the government's thinking. But it soon became clear that, actually, it did.

This ought perhaps to have been clearer earlier, because Wilkinson negotiated a unique deal with GTR when they took over their franchises in 2014. The other train companies operate like private companies. They get subsidies from the government, butthey also keep their ticket earnings, because that represents how successful they have been at attracting customers. The great advantage of privatisation is that it forces companies to be interested in what customers want.

Not so with GTR. They are paid a fee by the government - £8.9 billion over seven years and pay all the ticket receipts back to the government. The government even refunds all their payments shelled out to customers if the trains are delayed. There is no benefit in attracting more customers and no loss if GTR lets them down. They are simply government agents. It was not exactly how privatisation was intended to be.

Of course, they do still lose out if things go wrong. They have to pay fines to Network Rail for every minute trains are delayed, and fines of around £2,500 if they cancel trains. They have to pay fines to the Department for Transport if they fail to meet targets, and have done. They have to put in extra staff into their control centres, mainly in Three Bridges, to keep up with the chaos of their day-to-day schedules. That is why the profit of GTR was recently revised downwards from 3 per cent (presumably just under £40 million a year) to 1.5 per cent. No wonder Go Ahead's share price has been dropping.

Added to which, London Bridge remains a bottleneck, with knock-on effects throughout the network. GTR has found it difficult to retain staff, and made the mistake of making the very experienced controllers redundant at Three Bridges when they took over the franchise. And of course the stresses are mounting on staff and managers alike, face with enraged passengers, complex and rapidly changing cancellations, and a fleet of rolling stock which is also operating close to capacity. Their contract sets out that 96 per cent of carriages have to be used, when the normal industry rate is 85 per cent. That means that, again, if anything goes wrong – if there isn't enough time for maintenance or if one of them breaks down – the knock-on effects are immediate.

It is the same with staff. Total efficiency isn't actually very efficient in practice. There needs to be some spare capacity for the system to work effectively. Small organizations know that. It may be that most managers at GTR understand it too. But governments have a way of demanding the impossible and believing that, just by ordering something, they can make it so. It never is like that, but they are too far from the front line to see it.

The countdown to meltdown speeded up at the beginning of 2015 when major changes were introduced to the timetable, which tried to push too many trains through the tight bottleneck of London Bridge. GTR's performance dipped immediately by between six and seven per cent. The knock-on effects on a system that was already overstretched have never quite been resolved, though the timetable has been redrafted again.

Into this unwieldy situation, Aslef and RMT – the two main rail unions – threw in their bombshell in November, signing their agreement to accept no more driver-only operations. GTR managers told me that they believe their relationship with trade unions were good before that. But even if that was true, the 'concordat' made some kind of confrontation inevitable.

Gearing them up for the inevitable, the government intervened to support GTR managers in the coming battle. GTR was by then already the least successful franchise in terms of timekeeping, and public opinion was stirring. Backbench Conservative MPs were making angry noises after complaints from their constituents.

But ministers had decided they were going to back GTR. Officials wanted a victory, after all. The push for driver-only was coming primarily from Department officials – GTR was their champion in the lists, so to speak. They wanted to win.

So, in February this year, the Department announced a 'remedial plan' for GTR which would cut them some slack, aware that the coming confrontation with their staff would mean disruption. The plan allowed them to cancel another 9,000 trains in the year (to July, I believe) before paying penalties. In fact, the number of cancelled trains has risen already by 18,000 even by June.

As the days ticked by before the two-day strike in April, and then the one-day strike in May, the two sides negotiated successfully to reduce the impact on passengers. Charles Horton issued a tough letter to staff before the April 26 strike, which threatened to deduct two days pay (£268) for each day they withdrew their labour and a range of other sanctions.

The strikes went ahead, though there was enough trust between the two sides to change the timings to reduce disruption to passengers. That meant that Horton had to make good on his threats which had, arguably been unwise. As we have seen, these embittered relations with staff, which goes some way to explaining that the disruption has not really stopped since the strikes, even though there is no industrial action going on (though as I write, RMT is equally unwisely planning some more).

"This is money you will not recover," Horton had warned in his letter. "And when the RMT eventually try to settle the dispute, please be assured that GTR will not recompense you or waive any of the conditions covered later in this letter."

What most embittered the staff when they came back to work was not so much losing two days pay for every day they had been off, it was having their parking permits and the free rail travel for their families taken away from them. Free rail travel for families has been a perk of working on the railways since time immemorial and staff really minded this. It also meant that getting to work at all suddenly became extremely expensive, and – with the rail disruption – sometimes impossible.

There was also a ban on swapping roster duties to fit in with family arrangements. It may be that this was far more important than removing car park and family rail travel permits. It was almost, but not quite, enough to explain the cancellations – if your children need taking to the doctor, and there is no way to swap, it may explain, if not entirely excuse calling in sick. One of my correspondents put it like this:

"Even more destructive from the point of view of covering trains, they have stopped the guards from swapping duties with each other (something they have done since the beginning of time) Some guards don't have cars, they use the train to get to work, normally they swap very early starts or late finishes with other guards so they can simply get to work, but this vile company have said local managers must not allow this anymore thus causing more train cancellations. Guards have racked up taxi bills exceeding their wages just trying to get to work."

Again, this was difficult for an outsider to understand. The swapping was known inside the company as MCOs, which did initially confuse me. MCO is the acronym for many things, including Orlando Airport in Florida, but it also stands for 'Mutual Change Over'. By 15 June, the company had agreed that this was one inflexibility too far. They reinstated the roster swapping.

The company "listened to conductors", their chief operating officer Dyan Crowther told me, and allowed crews to swap rosters again. There was an immediate improvement in the train reliability, but the cancellations still carried on.

GTR's managers also seem to have considered banning overtime by train crews who had been on strike, so that they could not claw back their lost money. But this measure did not last more than a few days in April. In that sense, GTR has been correct that they have not banned overtime – though many train staff clearly believe that they have. More on that in a moment.

The first reaction of the company when they saw the sick rate rising was to release the data, so that the media called it a 'sickie strike'. The sick rates had certainly gone up, but there is really no evidence that this was anything more than it seemed – a reaction of stress, rage, misery, disillusionment and frustration.

The company has made a great deal of the unwillingness of train crew to come in on their days off, in return for another ordinary day's pay. But once you see the reasons in black and white, it is hardly surprising – especially without free parking – that they might not want to do so as much as they did. The truth is that GTR had been unwisely relying too much on crews coming in on their days off, and when they were a little more reluctant to do so, the tipping point – when everything began to unravel – was not far away.

One message I received from a guard shed some light on what that tipping point means in practice:

"The conductors have tried their best to do the extra work required but are now burnt out, stressed by the abuse they're getting from management as well as the abuse from many customers day in day out. Other front-line staff are now bearing the brunt from the cancellations and it's only a matter of time before other grades start to crumble - and that's before the threats to conductors over DOO (Driver-Only Operation), drivers balloting for action because they feel an extension of DOO is unsafe, and the threats against ticket office staff with the 'modernisation plans'. Not forgetting of course the platform staff, trying to maintain a service where trains suddenly get cancelled with hundreds of extra people dumped on a platform, no staff to move the train so it's blocking a platform, and the lack of 'on the spot' managers who can make decisions and the lack of information from Control who don't seem to know what is going on either because they have to try and work out what to do – all the while staff trying to answer customer queries about how to get to where they're going and being shouted at by customers who are being fed the 'sickness' lie."

Personally, I had not been seriously inconvenienced by the slow unravelling of Southern, because I only travel to London once a week. I was aware that the journeys were getting increasingly unreliable, but it was only on 8 June that it became intolerable for me. That was when I had my first conversations with Southern staff. The following day was even worse and, by the following Monday, only 13 per cent of trains were arriving within the regulatory four minutes 59 seconds on the London-Brighton line.

What staggered me after I wrote my first blog, and followed it up with what seems in retrospect rather an inflammatory open letter to Charles Horton, was not so much the rage it unleashed, but how little this collapsing service was being noticed around the country. Was it because this was somehow so mundane, so ordinary, that the media was failing to pay any attention? Or was it because it wasn't in London? And what can you do if nobody is paying any attention because this isn't happening in the metropolis? What do you do when the investigative journalists have mostly disappeared, along with the trains?

It was hardly as if I had any great expertise in the railway world. I was just equipped with a strong sense that the phrase "temporary staff shortages" which accompany every cancellation wasn't strictly accurate. As a result of the first blog I wrote, the messages began to pour in, on email and twitter, some anonymous, some logical, some incoherent with rage, leaked memos, quotes, facts, messages from company directors motionless at Clapham Junction, from guards, drivers and administrators. I had a poignant message from a disabled passenger unable to travel because he could no longer phone ahead to ask for a ramp when the trains never arrived.

Most people are still unclear what to do. Who is responsible, after all? Commuters chanting at plush South Croydon was pretty unprecedented but seems unlikely to rattle the government's resolve. The demonstration at Brighton was fun, especially when commuters chanted "No more lies" while the station manager was being interviewed on local television, but in some ways demonstrations and chanting simply emphasise your powerlessness.

Brighton has become an epicentre of the crisis. One person sent me a message explaining that there had been so many abandoned passengers on Brighton's Platforms 1 and 2 the previous evening that the police had been called. "It really is a bit much to have to get coppers to stop users using your trains," they wrote.

I also became aware of lawyers documenting overcrowded platforms ready for the public inquiry. I knew of video projects, interviewing projects, documentary projects. I'll say this for GTR. They have unleashed not just misery and rage, but creativity.

By 13 June, the mood had changed. The previous week, South Downs MP Nick Herbert was having admonishing meetings with GTR, but still buying the 'temporary staff shortages' line. By 13 June, the media was almost interested. The BBC Today programme interviewed a local MP. The *Brighton Argus*, aware that their story about a pregnant passenger who fainted had been their most read story of the day, sent a reporter to chase down the rail minister Claire Perry in London at the Department for Transport offices in Horseferry Road.

That was the day they reported that: "More than 50 per cent of the Brighton mainline services delayed or cancelled. More than 800 trains across the network were more than ten minutes late, with more than 250 of those registered as 'more than 30 minutes late or cancelled'."

And on Thursday, GTR's Dyan Crowther was giving me an interview (though I'm not sure she would have done if I had not also been writing for the *Guardian*).Why the change?

Well, I would like to think it was partly that a new kind of journalism was in the air. Nearly 100,000 people had taken the trouble to read what I had written, partly on my own blog and partly on the blog of the New Weather Institute, the thinktank where I am co-director. I would like to think that, one of the reasons that GTR began to engage in public was that I urged them to, and people clearly responded. But I know that part of the reason for the interest was that David Cameron himself became embroiled.

The Prime Minister had been due to speak at a referendum debate in Hayward's Heath, the other epicentre of railway misery in recent weeks. Some reports suggest he waited for two hours at Victoria. It may not have been as long as that. Either way, he was forced into his car and arrived very late and furious. Sussex MP Sir Nicholas Soames took the Transport Secretary Patrick McLoughlin aside in the lobby of the House of Commons and warned him what had happened.

Prime Ministers who get stuck on trains are apt to change transport policies on the hoof, as Margaret Thatcher is supposed to have done. But it was noticeable how the transport ministers defended themselves more aggressively afterwards. When *Argus* reporter Ben James tracked Claire Perry down, she was uncompromising and unapologetic, refusing to consider stripping GTR of the franchise. As far as officials are concerned, the rise in sickness at Southern has been a 'work to rule', not a result of poor management and a failure to stick to margins of error.

"I don't think changing the name on the company's front door would do anything to solve the problems," she said. "What I do think we have to do is sort out the industrial dispute, get the investment in there and get this back to being a high performing railway."

She then laid the blame entirely on the unions:

"It is absolutely right to get that new tech rolled out, but it doesn't mean there will be any fewer people on the trains.One of the great myths is that suddenly there will be only one person on the train.But the person whose job it is to open and shut the doors at the moment will become a customer services person. There will be no job losses, just better customer services.I think the union should take a really hard look at this. The union is holding commuters to ransom."

She also decided to defend the GTR managers calling them "top of the range".

Ben James asked her how she would like it if she didn't get to see her children at night because of rail disruption. She said: "It would be terrible ... That is why it is so important for the union and company to sort this out. Brighton commuters don't deserve a summer of discontent."

Of course, it isn't just Brighton commuters and the phrase 'summer of discontent' appears deliberate. Was she trying to encourage that onto the front page? In fact, what was on the front page was a picture of herself under the headline 'WANTED FOR INCONVENIENCING COMMUTERS'.

Which brings us to the original question which brought me into this whole tangled, complex web. Had the company actually banned overtime or not? If they had banned overtime, that would have been clear and unambiguous evidence that the company preferred to punish their staff more than they wanted to run an effective service – and that was what I had originally been told. A number of staff members who responded to my blog confirmed that this was the case.

But when Dyan Crowther called me on 16 June, she was pretty unambiguous that it was not true. It was, she said, "a complete lie". "We took the decision that we didn't want to do that," she said. "We took a clear decision not to impose an overtime ban."

She said the same on the Today programme on 17 June, once the extraordinary scenes on Southern had become national news. She said there had been "a reduction in the willingness of drivers to undertake overtime".

I have been given figures which show that there were 327 guard duties covered by overtime since 26 April (until 16 June), compared to 482 in the same period the previous year. So, yes, overtime, has been going on – but why so little?

There is a real problem for any outsider to

know the truth about this in the face of such an extraordinary contradiction. Understanding the inner workings of a company and the relations between management and staff is a bit like understanding a marriage. There is a whole culture to get your head around and it isn't easy. To find out, I went to see a working guard on their day off.

That experience, and a number of other conversations, have convinced me that my original interpretation was not as accurate as it should have been. In the strict sense, the company had not banned the strikers from doing overtime, though Dyan Crowther may have overstated the 'complete lie' line.

In some ways, it was worse than that – they had tiptoed into a delicate situation, with sanctions and reforms, without realising how fragile the delicate balance was that they were relying on. It wasn't deliberate. It was all a terrible error.

I must admit that Dyan Crowther's absolute determination that the overtime ban was a lie did confuse me. I could not understand why I was being told such contradictory things. Then something happened: I was leaked a document, which I did not fully understand at the time. It was only when it was leaked to the *Brighton and Hove News* that I began to grasp the truth.

The document is a memo to managers from the guards manager Piero McCarthy. It is undated but must have been issued sometime around 21 April. The main message is about the ban on MCOs, which – as I explained – is the ability of crews to swap duties if they need to for family reasons, as long as both agree. But across the top were scrawled these words in capital letters: "NO RDW A/Rs ONLY TO BE USED FOR NO COVER."

These require some explanation too. RDW means 'Rest Day Working', in other words overtime in other words. A/Rs are the As Required roster crews who are on stand-by. The instruction appears to mean that they would not have overtime, but to use the stand-by crews to cover instead.

As we have seen, keeping train crews on stand-by seems inefficient to managers but, of course, it allows them to plug sudden gaps and to deal with disruptions. GTR is a centralized company and finds these balances hard to understand, and they have increasingly been using the stand-by crews to cover for illness or absences. Since there are always some crews sick, that means that the vital buffer for emergency cover is rarely there.

The memo appears to imply that they intended to use the stand-by crews to cover for overtime on a more systematic basis.

The company defended itself by saying that the words in the leaked memo had been taken out of context:

> "The featured email has been taken completely out of context and comments made about it in your article are wrong. At some of our conductor depots individual managers had allowed conductors to work part of a shift on overtime, but be paid for the full shift. This is clearly not acceptable and the email is about putting an end to this practice. Nothing more."

But Dyan Crowther was still telling the truth. They may have discussed extending this 'sanction' against striking crews, but decided against it. If the injunction against 'rest day working' ever became a reality, it lasted no longer than ten days at the end of April. It is certainly not in place now.

But, as we have seen, they did introduce a number of other sanctions and reforms which had the effect of making what was a flexible local system into an inflexible centralized system. This happened in three important ways:

- Former strikers were prevented from swapping their rosters for family or other personal reasons. This sanction ended on 15 June.

- They were made to surrender their free parking permits and the free rail travel passes used by themselves for leisure and their families, which made it much harder – and sometimes more expensive – to get to work.

These sanctions "were proportionate to the disruption that the strikes were causing to the travelling public," Dyan Crowther told me.

But the company's response to the leaked letter had revealed this other sanction. They had ended the local arrangements whereby depot managers might agree to pay a whole shift for crews coming in on their days off to cover for absent colleagues for part of a shift, even though they might not do the whole nine-hour shift. It is this arrangement that GTR said was "clearly not acceptable", and was referred to in the leaked memo.

They said it was "nothing more", but this in itself is significant. They have put intense pressure on the depot managers to persuade crews to work on their days off. They are not allowed to pay extra for this overtime, but they did sometimes get them to come in to help for part of a shift, by agreeing to pay them for the whole shift.

This was a critical flexibility for the depot managers and it got the job done. Ending this must have seemed streamlined for senior managers, but in practice it has led to the collapse in overtime. It might even explain why so many of Southern staff assured me that 'overtime' had been banned. The truth was that overtime was still available, but paid the same as any other work (except for a small increase on Sundays) – but the little perks and leverage which used to persuade to work on their days off were no more.

From an outsider's point of view, it was this small change which made such a big difference.

The central problem is that, partly for reasons of efficiency, partly because they have not yet trained enough drivers, the system relies on drivers coming in on these days off and doing extra shifts. It means the company is always facing a basic unpredictability: overtime has to be voluntary. If eight of the 40 drivers at the Brighton depot are off on any given day, either sick or on holiday or retraining for the new Class 700 trains, then train managers will need to persuade other people to come in.

The difficulty is that this tends to be a last minute business. The depot managers will try and prepare for it by knowing who isn't going to be there and who might cover on their days off. If they don't, they will have to start phoning drivers at home to cajole them in. Often, the information fails to reach the control office, which cancels the train – so the driver gives up his day off, only to find the train he was supposed to drive has been cancelled.

"I must point out that this is nationwide practice and not a Southern rail specific practice," wrote a driver to me. "But it is [taken to] an extremity on Southern. Unfortunately, what you have in Southern at the moment is such a low staff morale [that] people are unwilling to come into such a toxic environment on their days off, meaning a larger number of jobs uncovered then usual. Staff don't even want to be there when they are supposed to be let alone when they don't have to be."

The rule is also that drivers need to have a half hour or two twenty-minute breaks on their shift. During disruption, which is now every day of course, the drivers are under pressure to waive their break to take out desperate passengers.

Then of course, you might have a driver scheduled to take over the train at Gatwick, and if they are off – and there is no spare capacity (and there isn't) – then the train gets cancelled at Gatwick. Because the first driver is required to take a different train back to London, and if he fails to show up that would be cancelled instead.

"Our workday is so tightly packed there is no room for any problems," writes one driver. "If we didn't have such tight schedules there would be more flexibility for when such issues arise."

There is the central problem. A highly centralized company was much more reliant on the goodwill of crews to work their days off than they realized. That made the system of cajoling staff to help that much more inflexible – when what they really needed was flexibility and informality. And leadership.

That was not, of course, what Dyan Crowther was asked about on the Today programme on 17 June, and very sensibly avoided the trap set for her in the interview by Justin Webb when he asked her why fully-crewed trains were being cancelled. As we have seen, the answer to that is highly complicated and she could soon have lost her way completely in the detail.

It was an assured performance, but it did not explain quite what was going on, even so. It did not explain the new inflexibility when it came to persuading train crews to forego their days off, and it did not recognize the pain involved in the whole business.

The real insights into stories like this come, not so much from the statistics, but from messages and postings which provide a human take on what it feels like. This one, from a Southern guard on an online bulletin board, moved me – and made it clear that much of the staff reaction has been emotional, and in an entirely understandable way:

"So my letter arrived. It seems sometime around 20th August, I will be getting my 12 weeks notice. I will then have 4 weeks to decide if I want to either: go on the dole, or be an OBS [Onboard Supervisor]. Sadly, not much of a choice. I also got another letter telling me that, since I went on strike, I need to hand in my car park pass and rail pass. Should make getting to those 4am starts and coming home from 2.30am finishes a bit more complex... I'm off this week on a block of rest days, so it's been nice to get away from it all. Funny thing is the latter asking for passes back, came the day after I had a person need urgent medical treatment. We waited for 30 mins at Plumpton station for an ambulance (on the ambulance services advice), but I made sure that everyone on the train got home on one of the last trains. All the punters seemed ok, with a few going, glad you're here, and so on. So for a tiny moment I thought the letter in my pigeon hole might have been a 'thanks'. But then I remembered who I work for. Oh well..."

III

The message

"There are many parts of the country, at certain times of the day, where customers really value a human presence on the train and there is real evidence where you de-man the railway it's affecting revenues adversely because it's seen to be less safe."
Peter Wilkinson, Director of Railway Franchising at the Department for Transport, 2009

I have set out the background and told the story, and I have done so in as balanced a way as I can. As far as possible, I have chased down this overtime ban story and I think I have finally pinpointed the truth. But there are still a number of very peculiar elements.

The first is that, although I may have been wrong that GTR was deliberately messing their customers about in order to 'sanction' their staff – as they put it – but they were behaving in a way which might reasonably appear like this. They were building inflexibilities into the overtime system when they were actually relying on it being flexible and informal. They could have run a more efficient service, and they did put extra resources into the control room – and they did let staff carry on swapping duties when they needed to – but they seemed unable to grasp how close to the tipping point they had become.

In the end it was more important to them to tighten their control over their staff than it was to get the trains to run effectively. They could have sunk their differences, but they were either not allowed to, or failed to see the opportunity. Perhaps they simply failed to diagnose what was happening accurately. They convinced themselves that their authority was under attack, and that never really leads to management clarity.

There were other peculiar elements too.

First, because this is not London, the media did not try to ferret out the truth and put it on their front pages, and ask why the company directors are drawing down government subsidies (£8.9bn over seven years) while they are failing to provide the contracted service. The *Brighton Argus* acted in the end. The Today programme responded belatedly, but generally there appear to be no journalists empowered to turn up at the depot and ask questions for themselves.

This book is an experiment in publishing, researched, written and published in the space of a week, but it should not have been necessary. Also, I'm all alone. I have no back up; no office. This maybe the modern world of news – but it shouldn't have had to be me.

Second, there have been questions in Parliament, but there was precious little political activity until 13 June. There is now an all-party parliamentary group to keep tabs on GTR's performance, jointly chaired by Hove MP Peter Kyle and Mid Sussex MP Sir Nicholas Soames. But for far too long the political world has been prepared to give GTR the benefit of the doubt.

Third, there are important questions here about the future of public services, given that privatisation now appears to have a different purpose – and it barely seems to have anything to do with competition. Are there any circumstances, short of outright criminality, where a private contractor can have the quality clauses invoked to lose their franchise? Is there no level of incompetence where the regulator will step in and act in defence of the customers?

Because if so, that isn't what privatisation was supposed to be about. It was supposed to be about providing a competitive market, to force utilities to be sensitive to the needs of customers – the precise opposite of what has happened with Southern Rail. It isn't clear to me what the difference is between a featherbedded public monopoly and a featherbedded private monopoly – clearly there are no competitive or regulatory pressures on GTR.

The argument against privatisation is partly that the profit required by investors, and by the contractors themselves – the huge salaries and bonuses they pay themselves at board level – is not an efficient use of resources. This is true, and it can only be justified if their specialist expertise provides savings, efficiencies and flair that outweigh those extra costs.

I am no great fan of old-fashioned state control, but one of the tragedies of privatisation has been that – far from being experts in delivery or enterprise – the contracting companies are often experts in delivering target data. If they have a common characteristic, they are companies that believe decisions can be based on this data – which often bears little resemblance to frontline reality, and who think they can run these empty shells as vast, vacant and inhuman machines.

In effect, that means that too many services

have shifted from sclerotic state control to sclerotic private control. Railway privatisation has been hugely successful at levering investment into the railways. They have not been so successful at running those railways effectively. Ironically, one of the most successful periods of any railway was the turnaround of the North East Mainline franchise when it was briefly back in state control.

There is an even more urgent problem for us, who are involved in public services as users. What can we do when things go wrong? We have no democratic levers – the government has been clear it will not intervene in GTR (not yet, anyway). We have no commercial levers – this kind of corporate giantism means they are pretty immune to financial pressure from customers, even if we had the choice to use them or not.

That is why the Southern meltdown is potentially so important. GTR and the RMT may believe that it is a watershed for them; it may turn out that, really, it is the moment that ordinary people develop for themselves some way of having some clout over the services they depend on.

The American historian Barbara Tuchman set out

in a classic passage about British military failure against the Japanese in Burma in 1942, which says a great deal about the postwar failures of British management:

"No nation has ever produced a military history of such verbal nobility as the British. Retreat or advance, win or lose, blunder or bravery, murderous folly or unyielding resolution, all emerge clothed in dignity and touched with glory. Every engagement is gallant, every battle a decisive action, every campaign produces generalship hailed as the most brilliant of the war. Other nations attempt but never quite achieve the same self-esteem. It was not by might but by the power of her self-image that Britain in her century dominated the world."

It isn't outright snobbery which leads to this fatal blindness, though snobbery is clearly involved. The upper tiers of management support each other through an infuriating, wordless silence. They do so largely through wilful ignorance. They close their eyes to the front line – they may never have been there in a working capacity – and believe that, if you put the incentives in place for the next tier below them, everything will come right. They have lost the art, which was later nurtured in the military, of inspiring those they lead.

This is why, when things genuinely go wrong in England, the heads don't roll. If Lloyds of London was ruining the middle classes who were investing in them, if RBS was threatening the world's banking system, well then, let's just keep the stiff upper lip and ride out the storm – pausing only to congratulate the 'gallant' generals and directors for their 'decisive' action.

We have left the era when there were seven tiers of carefully demarcated dining rooms at the Cowley car plant, or when sandwiches were cut in triangles for the managers and squares for the staff. But we still have the basic attitudes that go with that, and it goes with a kind of fatal idea that all you need to do is to bash your workforce and reward your management class and all will come right. If you can eliminate the human element altogether, all the better.

They forget that, although human beings are irritating because they make mistakes and need paying and nurturing, they are also the source of imagination, problem-solving and the human relationships with customers that make the difference between an empty humming silo and a successful and attractive business.

I have never been invited into GTR's offices in Monument Street, with their high-backed chairs, but it shows all the signs of an operation that is too centralised, too distant, too much managing by numbers, and themselves too put upon by their own bosses and contract managers.

I have written quite often about centralized states and centralized management, notably in my book *The Human Element*. The problem, especially in organizations, is that the management tiers must be open to challenge from below, from customers and staff. GTR managers listened to the frontline enough to reinstate the systems of swapping shifts, but it is difficult to see how the decision can have been taken to remove that kind of flexibility in the first place.

And if GTR is showing signs of becoming an 'absent corporation' where nobody seems home, that is nothing to the knots which government officials have tied them up in. They have been contracted to start driver-only services which require new equipment, which Network Rail can't install yet. The Department for Transport set the contract deadline and get to fine GTR if they fail, but the DfT also owns Network Rail and decides its priorities. As one of my informed correspondents wrote: "You really couldn't make this up."

Nobody really wants to work for companies that are run from the centre, by the numbers, as if they were giant machines. They are inflexible and often rather brutal. People don't want to rely on them either, though of course they can make exceptions if they are exceptionally cheap. If there is one thing worse for customers than being lied to, day in day out, it is the thought of being a small, expendable dependent of a giant, dysfunctional machine with no emotions except greed and fear.

If you add in the Whitehall fantasy that, just by tweaking people's expectations, you can change the actual situation on the ground, then you have a seriously unpleasant situation. The Treasury often fails to understand the human limits, the brute reality. Because the Treasury is too remote from real life to understand such mundane facts. That means the Department of Transport is sometimes forced to behave in a similar way, and so are their contractors, and their managers too. Big fleas have little fleas upon their backs to bite them, and so it goes down the line.

But there *have* been human limits and a tipping point. And although GTR may claw the situation back this time, it does not bode well for other contracts in the future. Nor does it bode well for the same management style in other services.

If a big train depot has to manage 40 journeys a day, and people are off sick with stress and there are not anyway enough staff to cover the 40 jobs without relying on people coming in to work on their days off – then what are GTR to do? Nobody wants to have train crews on standby waiting for an emergency, watching television and being paid. But you need some over-capacity to make the system work. It is brute fact. It may be that we will be in driverless trains in half a century's time, but my interpretation suggests that we will not embrace an ersatz, human-free, isolating and isolated future.

It remains to be seen, but don't bet on it. "In a virtual world, we will long for reality even more," said the American philosopher Robert Nozick. There is such a thing as reality. It does well to remember that.

So what can we do? What can we do when the

business establishment runs the services and they are protected in their incompetence by ministers?

This is the question which has kept me lying awake at night since I became involved in the whole Southern meltdown. Especially if the media is not interested – partly, perhaps, because they buy the idea that this is a trade dispute. And trade disputes, like divorces, are notoriously difficult to unravel for outsiders.

GTR seems pretty well protected from conventional political pressure, just as they are protected from economic pressures. They are a monopoly. Most of us have no choice whether to us them or not.

Nor do I personally hold out much hope for the unions, as presently constituted. They seem wedded to symbolic, revolutionary gestures, as if this was Moscow in 1917, with waving flags and crowds and chanting – and strikes. Strikes which hurt the passengers just as much as the failure to run trains competently hurts them. In the end, the interests of the RMT and Aslef are different from those of the passengers, though it would help – if only they could grasp that – to align them more effectively.

You will have gathered if you have read this far that I don't really believe that demonstrations have much effect, except to act out our own powerlessness in symbolic terms.

I can think of only a few ways forward. Clearly GTR is nervous about any kind of civil disobedience, but this is extremely difficult to organize and may end up hurting the staff more than the managers. Angry commuters were taken away from Paddington Station in handcuffs in June and this would certainly increase the pressure on everyone involved. But the results would be unpredictable and I don't want to be the one taken away by the police. I'm sorry if that is cowardly but that is the way it is.

Human reality

The late, great Anita Roddick used to use the phrase 'take it personally', and it seems to me that constantly bringing the situation back to the human reality is still the only effective way of campaigning.

Like me, most passengers feel let down by the appalling service on the south coast lines since April, because they pay GTR quite large sums to travel regularly to London, when the company regularly allow them to miss business meetings, miss picking their children up from school, miss getting their family home by bedtime at weekends, miss their teachers' meetings. Like so many other people, crammed into your cancelled trains in the heat, they are cross.

That is the human reality. They are also cross because of all the rhetoric from government and managers alike about striking train crews in April "inconveniencing passengers". They were inconveniencing us to get at GTR, and then GTR appeared to be doing the same to get at them. Is there really any difference?

The real human question is one of loyalty. We, the poor neglected, customers, the people driven from cancelled train to cancelled train like cattle, are loyal to their train company. Partly this is because we have to be – there is no choice – but we, generally speaking, obey Southern's little regulations and get our heads around the complex ticket rules. We also pay them a very great deal of money. Southern owes us some loyalty in return.

Then there is GTR's staff. I'm not talking here about continuing disputes – and there are bound to be disagreements between staff and managers in a changing industry – but what I see every time I travel is brave, resourceful, patient staff, explaining to passengers what they believe is happening, with no information and under the most enormous pressure. Day after day. I see them heroically coping with the stress, never getting cross or raising their voices as the anger of customer begins to ignite. They are not the caricatures painted by rail minister Claire Perry.

I don't stand by everything I wrote to Charles Horton in my open letter to him (nor has he replied). But I do stand by this:

> "We have been debating nationally what being English means and at its best, it seems to me, that the English value loyalty above everything. So where is your return loyalty to your customers or your staff? Where are your senior colleagues? Because we English suspect that absence is a sign, not just of inadequacy as a manager, but that maybe they are nursing a secret contempt for staff and passengers alike."

These are, after all, real people, with real emotions and human needs, staff, managers and customers. They are all being put into an impossible position by the decisions of well-paid people in the government or the boardrooms. And taking it personally also means holding them to account, as human beings. So Dyan Crowther and Charles Horton should not be getting the whole weight of rage, but some should be shared out up to the chairman of Go Ahead, Andrew Allner. And up toClaire Perry, the rail minister, and all the rest of the interconnected, silent, invisible public service owners of the modern age.

Dangers

You only have to travel to the coast these days to see what the dangers are, and they are surprisingly stark in the world of health and safety. I stood on one frighteningly overcrowded carriage and the man next to me told the crowd that, if there was even a small accident, it meant this for us – and he drew a finger across his throat.

You can of course take health and safety too far, but it is strange nonetheless that the regulator – now called the Office of Rail and Road (ORR)– isnot worried about overcrowding. "Despite being uncomfortable, and at times making passengers feel unsafe, there is no conclusive evidence linking crowding on trains with anything other than low level health and safety risks to individual passengers," they say on their website. "However, we continue to review the available evidence of links between overcrowded trains and ill-health effects on passengers."

I had a fascinating message drawing my attention to this, and agree with them that –

although there is clearly an element of truth about the ORR position, which makes trains quite rightly different from buses – there does come a point when "you are unable to move, cannot reach a handrail, have no access to water, have inadequate/no aircon, are pressed up against a door/wall/other person, can't get to the loo, cannot see an escape route if there was a fire... It's just a *feeling*." The message goes on:

> "That seems to strange to me. It also has equality implications. If you are elderly/frail ... heavily pregnant, prone to panic attacks, can't stand for long periods, need access to the loo regularly etc., you might choose to avoid a crowded pub or public event as a matter of preference. But you might not (and should not have to) choose to avoid rail travel."

The platforms have also been dangerously overcrowded. I am aware of one lawyer in Lewes who is documenting the overcrowding ahead of the inevitable public inquiry when there is an accident.

Disability
The best way of making this point is to quote from

a reply I received from a wheelchair user:

"Apart from the endless cancellations falsely blamed on staff sickness, how are disabled people such as myself supposed to manage when there are no guards to operate the ramps, most platform staff having already been dispensed with? Stupid question I suppose. The simple answer is that cripples like me aren't wanted on Southern's trains. Management obviously considers us a liability.

"Every time I travel, I have to book 'assistance' at least 24 hours in advance, but there is seldom anyone available to provide that assistance, so again it falls to the guard to get me on and off the train, so what's the point in booking?

"On Monday this week (June 13), I travelled from Portslade to Eastbourne, and for once the trains not only arrived, but arrived on time. Usually they're cancelled, so again, what's the point in booking a journey on a train that doesn't run, or, worse, runs but doesn't stop at any stations?

"Portslade station, as always nowadays, was closed, having apparently been abandoned weeks ago, so no assistance there. What happened to the four people who used to work at this station? There was nobody at Brighton to get me off the train or onto the next one, so again the guards had to do this.

"We arrived at Eastbourne, where there were already two trains waiting at the platform, presumably cancelled, and again there was nobody available to get me off the train, so again the guard had to do it. Staff cuts. Train cancellations. Pointless bookings. Now there's talk of getting rid of the guards, so I won't be able to travel at all.

"I have nothing but praise for train guards and platform staff, even regarding some as friends, but where *are* the platform staff? Trains are potentially dangerous things, and to imagine you can run a rail network with drivers only, and unstaffed stations, is insane and result in fatalities."

Those who have suffered most in the failure to run a proper service have been disabled people. The company will now be asking them to book 48 hours ahead of any journey, which will be hard for them. But if the company is failing to keep to their own timetable, and failing to put in place either staff on platforms or on trains – some trains will

not have on-board supervisors during disruption –
then the outlook for disabled people is even
bleaker. This is not fair. It may not even be legal.

Whether or not these are campaigning or legal
approaches which will bear fruit or unlock some
kind of leverage on a company we need to be
effective, I don't know. I do know the question is
now an urgent one.

It goes beyond transparency – because
conventional target figures do not actually hold
large service contractors to account (they hold
them to the target which tend to miss the point). It
goes beyond Westminster politics. But we have
inherited a corporate state where we have no say
in the services we use, and we badly need to
develop some.

Postscript

"In general, take my advice, when you meet anything that is going to be Human and isn't yet, or used to be Human once and isn't now, or ought to be Human and isn't, you keep your eyes on it and feel for your hatchet."
C. S. Lewis

As we go to press, there are some signs ofimprovement, anyway for this phase of the crisis. The work at London Bridge will have come to some kind of fruition by the end of the year and that will have beneficial effects through the system.

The trouble is that I get the impression that nobody, not even GTR's senior managers, quite understand why this crisis arose. My interpretation is that it was caused primarily by their inability to see how their 'sanctions' against train crews who went on strike had made an overstretched system much more inflexible. It undermined the goodwill and face-to-face details in a system that relied on that to cajole crews to work on their days off. Nobody had willed it – not the managers, nor the staff. Both were overwhelmed by the chaos and the tipping point that was so rapidly reached, the perfect storm of sickness, fury, stress, under-resourcing and centralization that caused it.

Neither the managers, nor the company, nor government officials, nor the unions, have been able to step out of their tramline thinking to rescue the situation. It does not bode well for the future, either of the railways nor of other public services contracted at such a distance, in the same way.

I am unable to publish the whole of this message I received in case it identifies the sender. But it moved me and it seems to sum up the message of this book. It comes from a lifelong railwayman who says he has never taken a sick day off in his whole career:

> "I take my role and its responsibilities very seriously and I was proud to be in a customer facing position where I could assist, guide and indeed protect those on my care.
>
> "I wanted to contact you more on a personal level to say I am ashamed of how we at Southern are performing. I am completely at a loss as to why this remains the case and indeed it is deteriorating.

"Staff absence, as in all industries, is a minor contributor to the current state of affairs, however, vacancies continue to dominate cancellations. This is not helped by an increasing number of conductors and platform staff resigning as the stress for most of us is becoming a serious problem. A serious problem which inevitably has and will lead to an increase in long-term sick absence.

"A colleague of mine contacted me recently. He was in tears and clearly struggling to cope. The ban on overtime, car park permits being demanded back by GTR and the withdrawals of staff family travel privileges, simply drove him to report sick with diagnosed stress and depression. He also encountered financial pressures due to overtime ban and the company's abhorrent position on refusing all exchange of duties between staff. This in itself causes additional heartache when trying to juggle life's everyday challenges, for example childcare.

"Over the last few months, I can honestly state that on every train I have worked, I have being subjected to abuse of various descriptions, from the very aggressive and potentially violent to the passive aggressive. Every day I'm told: 'You're crap, your company is crap, why are you holding the hardworking public to ransom.

"As each day passes, I feel increasingly tense and, dare I say it, emotional. Why? I just want to do my job and not be held as being responsible for the significant shortcomings of those in charge."

That seems to me to sum up a crisis which is primarily a human one. The solution seems to be human too, but humane solutions are rare in situations where debts, contracts and organizations have become far too big. I hope we will learn from this, ready for the next time.

Acknowledgements

I am extremely grateful to everyone who has sent messages and letters to me in response to the blog, and everyone else who has taken the time to give me background and advice, especially extremely helpful support from people at Rail Futures, *Modern Railways* magazine and from the Campaign for Better Transport.I'm also very grateful to my new friends Summer Dean and Emily Yates, and to Summer also for taking the front cover picture – a glimpse of contemporary Sussex life. And of course to my wonderful wife and children, who have put up with my flurries of railway activity.

The mistakes are mine, but I hope they are forgiveable. This is a highly complex affair and I hope this book will spread more light on a fraught situation, because it is a genuine attempt to understand.

V for Victory

Read the introduction here...

It was 6 June 1941, at fifteen minutes past midnight in continental time, three years to the day before D-Day, as it turned out. The British were preparing to march into Syria and Lebanon, the Germans were preparing to march into Finland and Russia. The war was entering a terrifying new momentum of its own. Those who tuned into the English language frequency of the BBC European Service that night, listening across a Europe occupied by the Nazis, heard for the first time an unfamiliar military voice, claiming to be a someone called 'Colonel Britton'.

Britton spoke with calm and reassuring authority. Not for long either, aware that his listeners may be listening in difficult circumstances and that listening to British broadcasts would probably be illegal, he spoke for just over four minutes, and – for the year in which he went on the air – never more than eight.

"Here in London, in the midst of this war, we

still get messages and letters from across the Channel," he told the listeners, huddling round their wireless sets desperate to hear the programme *London Calling Europe*. "They come by all kinds of strange ways from France and Belgium, Holland and Denmark, and even from Poland and Czechoslovakia. There are so many of them that I've been asked once a week to reply to them. To us, these messages are inspiring. They show there's a remarkable toughness about the people of Europe – so tough that it'll take a lot more than these heavily armed but half frightened Nazis to kill."

Was this true? Was there a remarkable toughness about them? Neither Colonel Britton nor his colleagues knew, but they *hoped* there was. This was an experiment: that by asserting this toughness they would, in fact, call it into existence.

Actually, the man behind the voice was not military at all. It was Douglas Ritchie, a former *Daily Telegraph* journalist who was then Deputy European News Editor, nominally at the BBC, though actually control of European broadcasts had been made semi-independent from the BBC some months before. The V campaign which Colonel Britton was announcing was a joint project with his boss, Noel Newsome, and had been carried out in the teeth of opposition from the competing government agencies struggling for control of propaganda to Europe.

It was the beginning of an extraordinary freelance piece of broadcast propaganda, and it remains a potent memory today – a key element in theEuropean Service's (and by default, the BBC's) formidable wartime reputation, credited with capturing the imagination of the occupied people's of Europe, revitalising their morale and fostering what eventually became the various resistance movements.

In real life, Ritchie was somewhat shy and self-effacing and held no military rank. Nor did he actually speak with the explicit permission, either of the War Office or the Ministry of Information. Nor was it an inspiring moment of the war. There had been a brief moment of elation earlier in 1941, when General Archibald Wavell succeeded in taking Tobruk, since then there had been reverse after reverse. And the dark continent, under Nazi rule across the English Channel, was silently ominous. Ritchie himself wrote later of the "terrible quiet" from there. In practice, it was unclear whether anyone was listening at all.

Those of us who know a little about the history of the Second World War, and who know what was to happen, are all too aware of the ferocious resistance movements that were to emerge to challenge the Nazis. But then, in the early months of 1941, they knew no such thing – and nor, except in a few pockets of occupied Europe, did the resistance movements yet exist. The V campaign, launched officially that night, was a first attempt to shape them – to give people the confidence to think independently again, to so blow on the embers of morale among the defeated nations of western Europe that they might one day resist.

So much of the background to the V campaign is now forgotten – the vitriolic war over the radio airwaves for the hearts and minds of Europe, the bitter battles over radio propaganda fought inside the British government, and the extraordinary success of the European Service, when 15 million ordinary Germans risked a death sentence every day to listen to broadcasts from London. But the aftermath of the V campaign lives on in the very mythology of modern Europe.

Colonel Britton broadcast every week for less than a year – a mysterious figure, the subject of much speculation on both sides of the Channel. But the paraphernalia of the campaign remains with us still in so many ways – the idea of simple acts of resistance, Churchill's ubiquitous V sign, but more than that too. There is an element of V that was, in some basic ways, part of the founding myth of postwar Europe. It provided hope that, one day, Europe would liberate itself – as indeed it did.

This is the story of the pre-eminent moment in the forgotten wireless war, when a few journalists – with no experience of policy or espionage, and practically without permission – launched one of the most effective press campaigns in history.

V for Victory, by David Boyle, is now available on Kindle and paperback from Amazon

Other titles by David Boyle

Building Futures
Funny Money: In search of alternative cash
What is New Economics?
The Sum of our Discontent
The Tyranny of Numbers
The Money Changers
Numbers (with Anita Roddick)
Authenticity: Brands, Fakes, Spin and the Lust
for Real Life
Blondel's Song
Leaves the World to Darkness (fiction)
News from Somewhere (*editor*)
Toward the Setting Sun
The New Economics: A Bigger Picture (with
Andrew Simms)
Money Matters: Putting the eco into economics
The Wizard
The Little Money Book
Why London Needs its own Currency
Eminent Corporations (with Andrew Simms)
Voyages of Discovery
The Human Element
On the Eighth Day, God Created Allotments
The Age to Come
What if money grew on trees (*editor*)

Unheard, Unseen: Submarine E14 and the Dardanelles
Broke: How to survive the middle class crisis
Alan Turing: Unlocking the Enigma
Peace on Earth: The Christmas truce of 1914
Jerusalem: England's National Anthem
Give and Take (with Sarah Bird)
People Powered Prosperity (with Tony Greenham)
Rupert Brooke: England's Last Patriot
How to be English
Operation Primrose
Before Enigma
The Piper (fiction)
Scandal
How to become a freelancewriter
V for Victory
Lost at Sea

See also our website at www.therealpress.couk

19273082R00070

Printed in Great Britain
by Amazon